AF207042

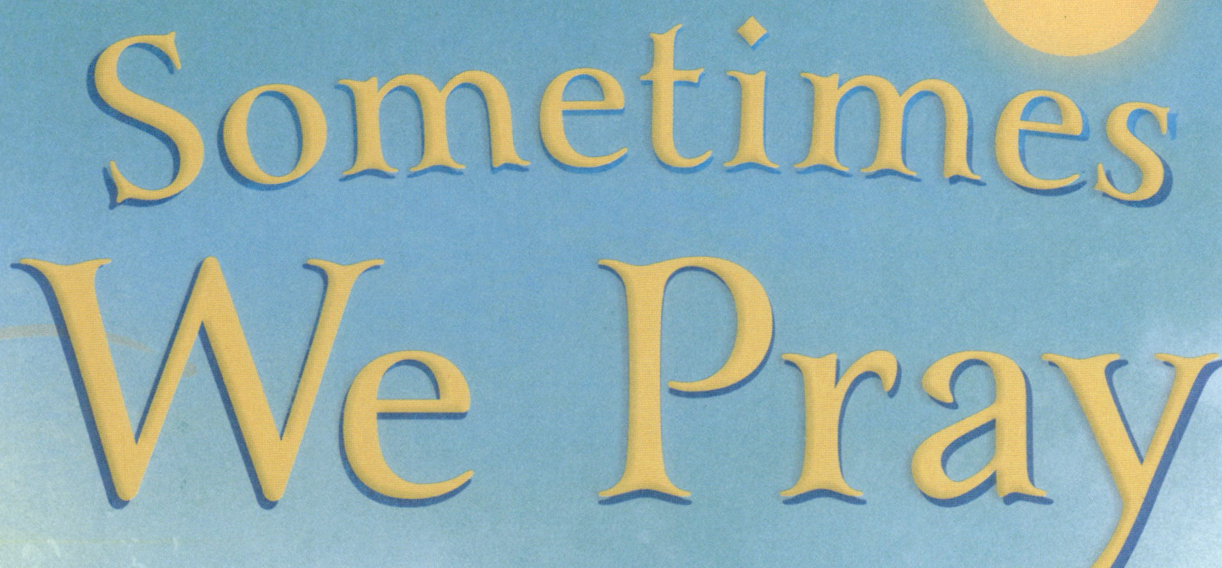

Sometimes We Pray

MARY WAGLEY COPP

Illustrated by
FELISHIA HENDITIRTO

Charlesbridge

Sometimes we kneel.
Sometimes we bend and bow.

Or lie flat.

We might pray with each step,

strumming each string,

inspecting each incredible leg,

or maybe . . .

marveling at a star.

Sometimes we pray with hands together.

Sometimes apart,
raised upward,
or close to our heart.

We might pray together
in a mosque or a meeting house,
in a temple, a synagogue, a church,

around a table,
or maybe . . .

in a meadow.

We may pray alone on a mat,

at a bedside,

by a gravestone.

We may pray counting beads

or turning a wheel,

sowing seeds or preparing a meal.

Or just waiting . . .

Sometimes we pray with eyes open to the sky,
to an altar

or by a holy site.

We pray with eyes closed, too.

We might pray in silence,
listening to the whir of the breeze,

the trill in the trees,
the purr in our lap.

Sometimes when we pray,
we sing and clap.

We chant,
dance,
and even weep.

We might rejoice and lift our voice
    to give thanks for our food, our home, and . . .

love, above all.

Sometimes we pray for forgiveness
and guidance.

To understand who we are.
Who they are, too.

To know we are not alone.

When things don't go our way, sometimes we pray . . .
for more rain,
for less rain.
For more kindness and peace.
Out there.
In here.

And for all the animals, too.

Sometimes we wonder if prayer works.
Someone we love gets sick . . .
and doesn't get better.

Someone is hungry or
doesn't have a home.

The rain doesn't stop or
never
comes.

But we keep praying, wherever we are.

We might be praying the same prayer,
sowing the same seeds, or . . .
marveling at the same star.

AUTHOR'S NOTE

One day, in the middle of an ELL (English language learners) class, two of my Syrian students stood up with their prayer rugs, went to a corner of the room, and knelt in prayer. Another student, a former pastor from Burundi, suggested that we sit silently as they prayed. The class obliged. A student from Haiti made a sign of the cross and others bowed their heads, as we sat in silence. When the class resumed, a lengthy conversation ensued—as best we could with the variety of languages we spoke—of what prayer meant to each of us. The curiosity of the students, coming from vastly different cultures, was heartening. In making space for, listening to, and hearing different perspectives, we found connection and discovered many shared values. *Sometimes We Pray* is inspired by that class. It is an offering to initiate similar explorations. During my research, many people shared their perspectives and practices, and I am grateful for their generous and open spirit.

GLOSSARY

Chanting: The sounds and phrases commonly used in spiritual practices. Chanting may be done alone or in a group. Diverse spiritual traditions consider chanting a route to spiritual growth.

Church: A building used for Christian worship.

Confession: In many religions, this is the acknowledgment of one's sins or wrongdoing.

Hymn: A traditional hymn is considered a formal song that is sung by a group of people gathered in public worship.

Labyrinth: A path that leads to a center, usually in a circular form. Many people walk labyrinths in silence and contemplation. For the Hopi tribe, the labyrinth symbolizes Mother Earth. The stone labyrinths along the Scandinavian coast were once used as magic traps to safeguard fishermen from trolls and dangerous winds.

Mala: A string of beads used for prayer and meditation by Hindus and Buddhists.

Mantra: A word, phrase, or sound repeated as part of a meditative practice.

Meditation: A practice in which an individual uses a technique—such as mindfulness, or focusing on an object or activity—to cultivate awareness and achieve a clear, calm, and stable mental state.

Meeting house: A place of worship and public meetings. Many religions, including Quakers (Society of Friends) and Mormons, congregate in meeting houses.

Mosque: A Muslim place of worship, also called a masjid. A mosque is the building where Muslims pray, but they can also practice Islamic prayers in any location.

Pilgrimage: A journey, especially a long one, to a sacred place as an act of religious devotion. Pilgrimage is an important aspect of some religions. Popular pilgrimage places are rivers, temples, mountains, and other sacred sites where the gods may have appeared or become manifest in the world. It's an undertaking to see and be seen by the deity.

Prayer wheel: A revolving cylinder inscribed with prayers, used by Tibetan Buddhists. Each turn of the wheel symbolizes the repetition of a prayer or a mantra.

Rosary: A Roman-Catholic sacramental and devotion to prayer in commemoration of Jesus and events of his life. The term rosary, describes both a sequence of prayers and the string of prayer beads used to count the prayers.

Synagogue: A Jewish house of worship where religious services are held as well as gatherings and study.

Temple: A building devoted to the worship—or regarded as the dwelling place—of a god or gods, as well as other objects of religious reverence.

To my agent Charlotte, for her immeasurable contributions to children's literature.
To my editor, Eileen, for her unwavering support of both creators and readers alike.
And to the human spirit that thrives on love, hope and understanding.—M. W. C.

For my mother, the most prayerful person I know.—F. H.

And for our designer, Cat: thank you.—M. W. C. and F. H.

Text copyright © 2026 by Mary Wagley Copp
Illustrations copyright © 2026 by Felishia Henditirto
All rights reserved, including the right of reproduction in whole
or in part in any form. Charlesbridge and colophon are registered
trademarks of Charlesbridge Publishing, Inc.

At publication, all URLs in this book were accurate. Charlesbridge, the author,
and the illustrator are not responsible for the content of any website.

Charlesbridge • 9 Galen Street, Watertown, MA 02472
www.charlesbridge.com

LIBRARY OF CONGRESS CATALOGING-IN-PUBLICATION DATA
Names: Copp, Mary Wagley author | Henditirto, Felishia illustrator
Title: Sometimes we pray / Mary Wagley Copp;
illustrated by Felishia Henditirto.
Description: Watertown, MA: Charlesbridge, [2026] | Audience: Ages 3–7 |
Audience: Grades K–1 | Summary: "An exploration of the power of prayer
in people's lives, including those that are not part of a religion"
—Provided by publisher.
Identifiers: LCCN 2024058941 (print) | LCCN 2024058942 (ebook) |
ISBN 9781623546410 board | ISBN 9781623546403 hardcover |
ISBN 9781632892867 ebook
Subjects: LCSH: Prayer—Juvenile literature
Classification: LCC BV212.C637 2026 (print) | LCC BV212 (ebook) |
DDC 248.3/2—dc23/eng/20250529
LC record available at https://lccn.loc.gov/2024058941
LC ebook record available at https://lccn.loc.gov/2024058942

Printed in China • OPIC
The authorized representative in the EU for product safety and compliance
is eucomply OÜPärnu mnt 139b-14, 11317 Tallinn, Estonia,
hello@eucompliancepartner.com, +33757690241
(hc) 10 9 8 7 6 5 4 3 2 1

Illustrations done in digital media | Text type set in Urge by Eclectotype |
Edited by Eileen Robinson | Designed by Cathleen Schaad |
Production supervised by Jennifer Most Delaney